Swimming is great

**Written by
Miss Joyce**

**Illustrated by
Sarah-Leigh Wills**

Jean-Paul is going to his very first swimming lesson with his grandmother. He is excited, but a bit nervous at the same time.

While they wait at the bus stop, Jean-Paul asks Nanny Jeanine lots of questions.

"Will I have to put my face in the water? Do you think I will be able to touch the floor? What if I'm not as good as the other children?"

"Just try your best and have fun," she tells him, "some of the other children may be feeling the same."

Jean-Paul's friend Emily and her mum arrive at the bus stop just as the bus comes and they all get on together. Emily is going for her first swimming lesson too. She looks excited.

"Hello! I see that you are nice and early too," says Nanny Jeanine.

"Yes, I need to make sure that the swimming teacher has seen Emily's notes because Emily was born without her right arm," says Emily's mum. "We also want to watch one of the other lessons to get an idea of what we will be doing."

"We want to watch another lesson first too," Nanny Jeanine says.

Emily is excited. She tells Jean-Paul about her new costume.

When Jean-Paul and Emily arrive at the swimming pool, they see a boy from their school called Ezra, with his dad.

Ezra has been going to the pool during the school holidays with his family, to get used to being in the water.

Ezra explains to Jean-Paul and Emily that he has been practising blowing bubbles, and that his dad has bought him a float to help with his kicking.

"I can't wait to learn to swim, so that I can join the summer programme," Ezra tells them. "They use inflatables! It's for strong swimmers only."

"Come along children, let's watch the class before yours," says Emily's mum.

"Look, they are blowing bubbles, just like I told you earlier," says Ezra. "I can do that."

Jean-Paul looks a bit worried. "Nanny, I can't do that."

"It's OK," says Nanny Jeanine. "That's why we are here - for you to learn. Swimming is the only sport that could save your life, or someone else's, so it's very important for you to learn. Come on, let's go to the changing rooms."

"Can you help me to put my swimming hat on please, Nanny?" Jean-Paul asks.

"Yes, of course. Remember how we practised at home? Hold the hat just over your eyebrows with your fingers and thumbs, and I will hold the opposite end. Now tuck your hair inside your hat, and don't forget your goggles," explains Nanny Jeanine.

"Thanks, Nanny. Do you think the teacher will be kind?"

"Yes, she looks very nice," Nanny Jeanine reassures Jean-Paul.

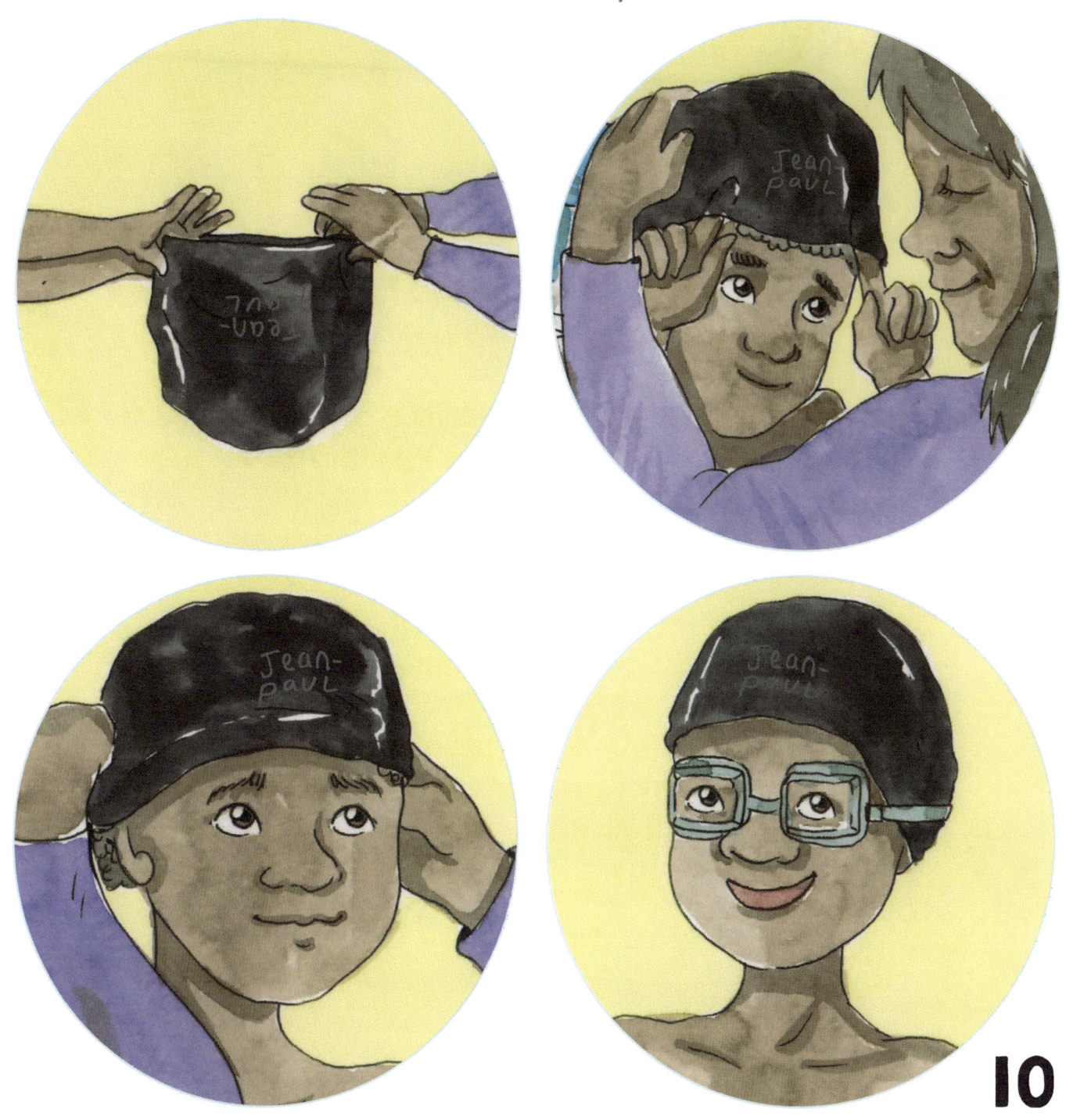

Emily has finished getting changed.

"I am ready, boys. Come on!"

"Wait!" says Jean-Paul. "Look at the sign! There are three rules to follow before we go onto the poolside."

The sign says: Blow your nose! Go to the toilet! Have a shower!

"Come on!" calls Emily, as she heads towards the toilets.

"Wow! The pool is big! Will I be able to stand up in the water?" asks Jean-Paul as they line up ready for the lesson to start.

"Shh! The teacher is here, we must listen," Emily hisses.

"Hello everyone, my name is Miss Joyce."

Emily's mum checks that Miss Joyce has seen Emily's notes.

"Yes, that's fine. Thank you for checking," Miss Joyce replies and she smiles at Emily.

"Now children, before we start, I would like you to listen to some very important rules," Miss Joyce tells the class.

"More rules!" Ezra whispers. "I just want to get in and swim."

Miss Joyce continues "There is no running on poolside and if you hear the alarm or whistle, stop whatever you are doing and make your way to the edge of the pool, please."

"Now, are we ready to get in?" asks Miss Joyce.

"Yes!" all the children call out.

"Please sit on the edge of the pool with your legs in the water and listen!" Miss Joyce tells the class.

"You are going to roll over onto your tummies one at a time and wiggle into the water like a caterpillar. You will all be able to stand up; the water will only come up to your chest," explains Miss Joyce.

The children do as they are told.

Jean-Paul is glad he can touch the bottom.

21

"Now, are we all ready to blow bubbles?"
asks Miss Joyce.

"Yes!" says Ezra loudly.

"OK, Ezra, you may show the class in a moment," says Miss Joyce, "Everybody, watch me first."

Miss Joyce shows the children how to blow bubbles and then Ezra tries.

"Well done," Miss Joyce says,
"that was good, Ezra."

"Now, we are going to hold onto the side and kick our legs while blowing bubbles," Miss Joyce explains. "Watch me first."

Miss Joyce shows the children what to do. At first, Jean-Paul finds it difficult, but then he manages to get it right and feels happy.

"Now, everyone pick up a float. We are going to try and kick to the other end of the pool. Emily and Ezra will try first," says Miss Joyce.

Jean-Paul watches Emily kick her way across the pool and is amazed at how good she is, despite not having her right arm.

"This is so much fun!" says Emily. "I can swim!"

"Nearly," says Miss Joyce.

Jean-Paul goes next.

"This is fun!" Jean-Paul cries.

"OK class, we have finished for today.

Everyone, climb out of the pool, please."
Miss Joyce tells them.

"Oh, can we stay in a bit longer?" asks Jean-Paul.

"I'm afraid not. I have another class now," explains Miss Joyce, "but I will see you all next week. If you want to, you can practise blowing bubbles in the bath at home, but you must have an adult with you. Or, you can come to the swimming pool with your family and show them what you have learnt."

The children walk to the changing rooms.
They have all had fun.

"I can't wait to go swimming again. My dad is going to take me at the weekend," says Ezra.

"I'm going to ask my mum if I can practise blowing bubbles in the bath tonight," Emily says, excitedly.

Nanny Jeanine is waiting in the changing room, ready with a towel and a big hug.

"How was the lesson, Jean-Paul?," asks Nanny Jeanine.

"I was a bit nervous at first, but once we started, it was great.

I didn't want to get out!

I can't wait for next week," says Jean-Paul with a big smile.

Read book Three to find out how Jean-Paul and his friends continue to enjoy their swimming lessons and how Jean-Paul overcomes his fears.

It's an exciting time for the children as they start to enjoy swimming without floats. Come and share their swimming adventure.

This book is dedicated to the most important person in my life: my Mummy.

Acknowledgements:

Thank you to everyone who supported me with my first book: I Don't Like Swimming, and with book two: Swimming is great.

Special thanks to Sarah-Leigh Wills for her wonderful illustrations.

A catalogue record of this book is available from the British Library.

First published 2020.

Written by Miss Joyce

ISBN: 978-0-9955765-2-0

All rights reserved.

No part of this book may be reproduced, copied, scanned or distributed in any manner whatsoever without written permission from the author, except in the case of brief quotations for critical articles and reviews.

© Copyright belongs to Joyce Dooknah

Illustration and Design by Sarah-Leigh Wills.

www.happydesigner.co.uk

© **Swimming is great** - 2020

Printed in Great Britain
by Amazon